Puppies!

Why Do They Do What They Do?

Real Answers to the Curious Things Puppies Do
with training tips

By Penelope Milne
Illustrations by Buck Jones

BOWTIE PRESS®

A Division of BowTie, Inc.

Ruth Strother, Project Manager
Nick Clemente, Special Consultant
Amy Fox, Editor
J. J. Smith-Moore, Designer
Michael Vincent Capozzi, Cover Design

Library of Congress Cataloging-in-Publication Data
Milne, Penelope, 1960-
Puppies! : why do they do what they do? / by Penelope Milne ; illustrations by Buck Jones.
  p. cm.
ISBN 1-889540-58-7 (pbk. : alk. paper)
1. Puppies—Behavior—Miscellanea. I. Title.
SF433 .M575 2000
636.7'07—dc21
      00-009223 00010252

BowTie Press®
A Division of BowTie, Inc.
3 Burroughs
Irvine, California 92618

Printed and Bound in Singapore
10 9 8 7 6

Contents

Why Do Puppies Like People?

People have lived with dogs for so long now that it's difficult for us to recognize the oddness of primate-us sharing our "caves" and lives with wolf-thing-predator-them. (But it is weird, when ya think about it!) Why do we do it? Why do they (other than that they have no choice, now)?

Clearly, humans have profited from our domestication of dogs. For thousands of years dogs have guarded, herded, hunted, and otherwise labored for us, while also entertaining and (it seems to us, anyway) loving us. During this time we have inadvertently and then deliberately genetically selected increased friendliness in dogs. Dogs are no longer wolves; our influence has created a huge change in the species, allowing dogs to form affectionate bonds with people.

Still, there is no guarantee that all puppies will like all people. In many cases, fear of people is caused by inadequate socialization: The puppy has not had enough positive experiences with enough people or enough kinds of people during her Sensitive Period for Socialization. Dogs are very good at noticing differences. They notice whether you are

wearing your running shoes *(Yay! Increased chance of dog walk!)* or your business clothes *(Aww...I have to wait through the boring time),* and they definitely notice differences in people. Often dogs wind up undersocialized to the kinds of people you (and therefore the puppy) don't bump into every day: for example, you see mostly adults, so the puppy fears kids.

Positive, active early socialization will make a big difference to a puppy's ability to enjoy the variety of humankind. But remember that behavior is the (still mysterious) product of genetics and environment, so, unfortunately, adequate early socialization, critical as it is, is not an absolute guarantee that the puppy will be free of behavior problems.

Why Do Puppies Urinate When They Greet People?

Urinating when greeting is a sign of deference, fear, or overexcitement on the puppy's part. A shy puppy's "piddle" response may be caused or exaggerated by what he sees as intimidating behavior from the big person in front of him. What kind of person would threaten a puppy? Well, a lot of perfectly nice people do it inadvertently. Dogs communicate with one another and with us mostly by using body language. Body-big postures such as looming, approaching directly from the front (rather than from an angle), making direct eye contact, or reaching over a puppy's head may all be interpreted by a puppy as threats.

Family members and visitors should be instructed to "ignore" a shy puppy at first—do not pursue or lean over him. When the puppy chooses to approach, he can be offered small yummy treats. The puppy can also be taught (in separate training sessions) to sit and to shake. Once the puppy starts associating people with Good Stuff, you can use the sit and shake commands to control both the person and the puppy in the greeting ritual. A person who crouches and reaches for the puppy's extended paw is no longer looming and reaching over the puppy's head, and the puppy has developed a substitute behavior pattern, one for which he has been rewarded many times and, therefore, has positive associations with.

Young puppies go through a *Sensitive Period for Socialization* during which they form social bonds. From about three to twelve weeks of age, they are sensitive to input from other dogs; and from five to twelve weeks, they are most sensitive to input from people. (Between weeks ten through twelve and sixteen through twenty, they are primed to investigate the environment around them.) Enriched socialization during this sensitive period can help prevent later problems. Give your puppy the chance to meet and get treats from a wide variety of people; interact with a lot of other healthy, sweet-tempered dogs; and explore safe new environments.

Without this socialization and habituation, there is an increased chance that the puppy will be fearful and possibly even fear-aggressive as an adult. The most common reason for dogs to growl or bite is fear.

Fearful dogs must feel as if they have very limited options—leave or make the Scary Thing leave. If the dog is on a leash or in a confined space when he is approached by someone he fears and cannot avoid, he is likely to snap or worse. A good, nonforce puppy kindergarten class followed by a good, nonforce basic obedience class are musts for every dog.

Why Do Puppies Jump Up on People?

Puppies probably jump up on people mostly to reach their interesting parts—hands and faces. Then the puppy's behavior is positively reinforced until, soon, jumping becomes a habit. A tiny puppy may be patted or picked up for jumping because *it is so sweet that the little cutie wants attention*. Later, when the puppy is older and bigger, jumping becomes a habit for the dog but an irritation or even a hazard for the humans. (Being smacked into a stucco wall by an enthusiastic five-month-old Lab who already weighs 50 pounds is no fun.) Even once they are irritated by it, though, people's responses to their jumping puppies may still serve to rein-force, not discourage, the behavior. Often the puppy is essentially ignored when she greets people quietly and politely but touched and talked to, or even shouted at—"Bosco! BosCO!, No, No, awwww...," when she jumps, so she continues to jump up.

Take advantage of the fact that dogs behave only in ways that work for them. Make sure that for your puppy, sitting-to-greet people works well. From the day you bring her home, she can be at first food-lured to sit, then later cued to sit-to-greet.

To teach your puppy to sit, hold a food treat (or other tempting lure) right at your puppy's nose, then move the treat toward her back and up in a small arc so that your hand with the treat is over her collar. The puppy will lift her head and drop her rear. As soon as she sits, praise her and give her the food treat. Once her response is smooth and predictable, give the verbal cue "sit" before you lift your hand to lure her. After a day or two of her following the lure, you should be able to get the puppy to target your empty hand, responding to the hand signal (your right hand, palm up, moving toward your right shoulder).

Once the puppy has a reliable response to the sit command and signal, practice greetings. Come through the door using the hand signal first, saying "sit" firmly as you greet the puppy. If the puppy jumps, do not knee, push, talk to, or touch her but instead immediately turn your back to her or even dramatically turn and walk back out the door. Wait a moment, then repeat the exercise again and again. The puppy gets the message that sitting works while jumping fails as an attention-getting or satisfying strategy. This practice should be repeated (and repeated!) with neighborhood kids, relatives, guests, etc. Puppies learn best from feedback that is clear, is consistent, and has been presented to them many times.

Why Do Puppies Mount Things?

Puppy owners, who are prepared for their little furry one to be cute, adorable, playful, and loving are often surprised that the puppy package comes with other elements too. Puppies growl, bite, eat really gross stuff (given half a chance), and, yes, they can show embarrassing interest in mounting people, stuffed toys (such as teddy bears), and especially one another. This behavior is entirely normal—puppies rehearse the behaviors they will need to use as adults. Mounting, even in adult dogs, is about social status (rank in the pack) as well as, or even instead of, being reproductive in function.

Dogs do not usually need human advice about mounting one another. They have excellent intraspecies communication. Humans need intervene only if there is a big size or temperament mismatch between the puppies or if a puppy is mounting an adult dog who is poorly socialized and therefore is incapable of gentle discipline. The puppy should, in general, be kept away from such crabby individuals.

You don't have to worry about how Mr. Teddy Bear feels about his status as "sex object," but, as with other behaviors, if the puppy's "enthusiasm" is bothering people, it is appropriate to say firmly, "Enough!" and then remove the toy and give the puppy a substitute activity such as chasing a stuffed BusterCube. It is never okay, however, for the puppy to pester humans by mounting them.

WAYS TO DISCOURAGE MOUNTING:

· Teach the puppy to sit and shake to greet people.

· Make sure the puppy gets a lot of attention in interactive games such as hide-and-seek and fetch, but reduce patting and touching that may get him overexcied.

· Have your puppy neutered or spayed. (Yes, females also mount but less often than do males.) Neutering by itself does not entirely eliminate mounting behavior—not surprising, really, since it is not a purely sexual behavior to begin with. Nonetheless, responsible puppy owners alter their puppies, protecting their pets' temperaments and health and helping to lessen pet overpopulation.

Why Do Puppies Lie under Tables?

If anybody knows the answer to this, it would be the puppies. But here is what we humans surmise: baby dogs feel secure in enclosed denlike spaces. Sleeping under the couch, in the kneehole of a desk, and upside down against a wall are all popular. Denning under the kitchen table has the obvious additional advantage of an increased chance of finding morsels of food!

The nice thing, from a human point of view, about puppies' preference for proxy dens is that puppies typically take well to being crated (being briefly confined to a plastic or wire kennel) when properly introduced with toys, treats, and initial short-duration visits. Crating helps prevent errors in housebreaking, chew training, etc. It protects the puppy, the human habitat, and the puppy's relationship with an owner who might otherwise be irritated with her.

Why Do Puppies Eat Dirt—and Snails and Leaves and Paper and. . . ?

Puppies explore the world in part with their mouths. They have a HUGE amount of learning to do before they become "sophisticated" adult dogs who are good (well . . . better, anyway) at telling the edible from the inedible. It is normal for even adult dogs to scavenge and try to extract calories from anything foodlike; eating three-day-old dead stuff and snails and so on is perfectly acceptable, necessary even, in dog society.

Of course, your puppy needs to be protected from himself while he is attempting to gain experience about the world. He should be either supervised, or, when necessary, temporarily confined to a puppy-proofed area with his own safe, durable toys so that he can make only good choices—that is to say, what we humans consider good choices, since the puppy already liked his choice: eating dirt!

It only takes a moment for a puppy to get into real trouble. Oh, you noticed that already? Here are some tips for puppy proofing your home.

Supervise:

- Gate off a (smallish) area of the house where you and the puppy will hang out together. (Don't isolate the puppy; do watch him.)

- Temporarily remove the most puppy-tempting and vulnerable possessions from the area.

- Remove hazards such as potentially toxic plants (ask your veterinarian for a list), dangerous chemicals from under the sink, and so on.

- Provide appropriate toys.

When you can't supervise, confine the puppy:

- Choose a crate, exercise pen, dog run, or dog-proofed room, depending on your puppy's age and potential for destruction and the necessary duration of the confinement. (An eight-week-old puppy left alone for two hours will probably do best if crated. A bouncy adolescent Lab left alone for five hours may do better in a dog run.)

- Be aware of your puppy's size—he may be little enough that he could come to harm by escaping through a tiny gap in an otherwise safe area.

- Provide some entertainment, for example, food-stuffed toys such as Kongs or a sterilized bone.

- If the puppy will be left for more than three or four hours, provide water, food if necessary, and a toilet area.

Why Do Puppies Eat Poop?

Even the well-fed modern dog continues to act like (indeed, continues to be!) the scavenger that she had to be to survive in earlier, harsher times. Many dogs will eat anything with calories in it—even food already processed once by the intestines (aka feces, or poop). Puppies tend to be even less discriminating than adult dogs are about what they eat. Usually, poop eating, coprophagia, is a normal, if unpleasant-to-humans, dog behavior.

If your puppy eats her stool, do check with your veterinarian to ensure that your puppy is healthy and that her interest in feces is not the result of any dietary deficiency (unlikely) or other medical cause. In some cases, coprophagia seems to be a result of boredom or stress. If the puppy is housed in a relatively empty, unchanging environment and lacks exercise, contact, and stimulation, she will certainly develop undesirable behaviors, one of which may be eating poop.

Many puppies grow out of eating their own feces. But if your puppy's problem is persistent enough to require treatment, try scheduled feeding and supervised pooping so that you can pick up the poop before the puppy gets to it. Also, try sprinkling Forbid powder (available from your veterinarian) onto the food of the animal whose feces are being eaten, making the stool produced as a result of that meal taste unpleasant to the puppy. Unfortunately, even though most puppies mature out of eating their own stool, eating cat "poop-sicles" remains popular with dogs throughout their lives. If you find that your puppy has been snacking out of the litter box, simply prevent her from getting access. Put a baby gate across the door of the room containing the litter box. Depending on how you set it up, an agile cat can go either over or under the gate, while the puppy is stuck on the other side. Prevent, don't punish. Punishment won't solve the problem and will only frustrate you and the dog.

Why Do Puppies Go Potty So Much?

Puppies have small stomachs, small intestines, and small bladders but high caloric needs and high energy (they move around A LOT), so their input/output cycles are very short. Generally a puppy can retain urine for the number of hours he is in months old, plus or minus an hour. A twelve-week-old puppy is about three months old, so he can probably "hold it" while crated or confined for about three hours, provided he has a chance to go potty first. Puppies usually have the same number of bowel movements a day as they have meals, so, for example, a puppy eating three times a day can be expected to have three bowel movements a day. (If your puppy is having many bowel movements or if his stool is very soft, consult your veterinarian. It may simply be that your puppy has a different "normal," or he may need treatment.)

THE PUPPY'S RULES OF HOUSEBREAKING:

- Puppies don't want to soil their eating or sleeping areas. They prefer to "go" in relatively large, open, unused areas of the house or yard. For example, it is common for a puppy to leave the kitchen/family room area to eliminate in the empty formal dining room, which must seem like the "wilderness" to a puppy.

- The more active a puppy is, the more he will need to eliminate. Especially, any change from inactive to active will make him need to "go," so after the puppy eats and drinks, plays, goes for a walk, or just wakes up, escort him to the toilet area.

- Puppies quickly develop a powerful "surface preference" and thereafter attempt to eliminate on their chosen surface whenever possible. So choose the puppy's "potty place" carefully. (Most dogs innately prefer to eliminate on absorptive surfaces such as grass, dirt, gravel, or carpeting, rather than hard surfaces such as concrete, tile, etc.)

- Watch your puppy carefully, take him out frequently, and confine him in a kind and safe way when you cannot watch him.

Why Do Puppies Chew Everything?

Puppies don't see the world the way we humans do, which when you think about it is not surprising. Why would they? But we are so used to living with dogs and considering them family members that we sometimes don't realize that puppies come to us without any pre-installed information about what humans value and why. In other words, of the various "dead-cow" objects in your family room, a rawhide, a Reebok, and a leather couch, how does a puppy decide which one to chew? Not by the object's human-assigned function, certainly. Puppy criteria might be, *something small enough to drag away like prey and clearly of value to my (human) pack mates,* as demonstrated by the humans having put their scent all over the item. In other words, the smelly sneaker would be the number one dog choice! She might chew the couch (especially if she were resting her chin on the arm, so the "chewy-couch" was right there under her teeth) and, yes, she might enjoy the rawhide, but it is not reasonable to expect the puppy to guess in advance what choice her humans would like her to make. It is essential to supervise the puppy and gently teach her. She will eventually learn those odd human rules!

Why Do Puppies Act Scared by Loud Noises?

Dogs, as one would expect of a species with a genetic heritage of being predators, are sensitive to any sudden environmental change. And, of course, their senses of smell and of hearing are so much more acute than ours that they have more to process and therefore have more to worry about.

A dog often spooks at the sudden appearance of a person or object, barking at someone who steps out from a doorway or who is suddenly noticed at twilight. Puppies routinely spook at the sound of something being dropped or a distant *bang*. Also scary, seemingly, is the sudden appearance of the Goodyear blimp or a kite or any other weird object in the sky. Even a street sign rattling in the wind bothers many puppies.

This behavior that seems unreasonably spooky to us humans was hugely protective and therefore valuable to our puppies' wild ancestors. *Run first, check it out later* is a sensible action plan for a wolf encountering a *Scary Thing*. In our pet dogs we have gradually produced animals with a higher degree of confidence and sociability than was present in their wild ancestors, but, still, some dog breeds—notably the herding and guarding breeds—if undersocialized and underhabituated to a diverse environment—are likely to show fear.

At home, habituate your puppy to sounds by banging those pots and pans and singing loudly while offering the puppy treats. Yup! You spotted it—it is the Italian Kitchen Effect!

Part of responsibly raising a puppy is exposing him to novel sights (and sites!) and sounds without overwhelming him, of course. Puppies should attend a gentle puppy kindergarten class, where they will be exposed to new stuff, and where the instructor will counsel the humans about managing behavior and preventing problems.

A GOOD CLASS FEATURES:

- An experienced, friendly, helpful instructor. Look for a trainer who is an Association of Pet Dog Trainers (APDT) member. (Web site: www.apdt.com);

- Nonforce methods;

- Training that is fun for people and puppies;

- Small class size;

- A curriculum based on real-life situations, not obedience trial exercises;

- Temperament training and behavior problem prevention and solving, in addition to command response training.

Why Do Puppies Play Keep Away?

Puppies play keep away because it is so incredibly fun! Let's look at it from a puppy's point of view: First, you pick your desired object (your trophy) according to your assessment of its social value, that is, who else seems to want this thing *(What has my person's scent all over it?)*. Then, you test your object. If you parade past your humans carrying a pair of underwear (specially selected from the laundry basket) in your mouth, will they all shout your name and play with you, chasing you round and round, eventually ending the encounter with a satisfying game of tug-of-war? Yup, they do! What fun! The only conclusion you as a puppy could draw is that you should repeat this game as often as possible!

Now, let's see what happens if you parade past your people, mouthing your Nylabone. Nothing. No attention. Nobody gets up. Nobody plays tug-of-war. What a dud! You would rapidly decide not to waste time carrying dog toys around.

So, what are you (as a human) to do when your pup continues to play keep away with inappropriate objects?

1. Ensure that your puppy has a set of toys she enjoys:
   - Retrieving items (aka stuff she can chase);
   - Safe shakable toys (aka stuff she can "kill" by breaking the furry thing's neck) such as a rope-bone or stuffed toy (if safe for your individual puppy);
   - Toys stuffed with food (a hugely popular category with dogs) such as a stuffed Kong, rope, bone, food ball, or BusterCube.

2. Carry around any new puppy toy for a day or two before letting your puppy have it.

3. Flatter the heck out of your puppy every time she plays with her stuff.

4. Encourage the puppy to play fetch.

5. Puppy Proof and Supervise! The puppy should not have access to people stuff she could steal.

6. Teach "I'm gonna get you" as a command so both running away with items and returning with them are seen by the puppy as worthwhile, rewardable activities.

7. At a quiet moment, teach the command "give":
   - Say "give," then give the puppy a yummy treat in trade for a low-value (i.e., boring) item. (For example, give her beef jerky for her nylon bone.)
   - Gradually increase the value of the item the dog has (say, a beloved toy and then your favorite shoe) that you are trading for;
   - Always use the same command (give);
   - Always say the give command just once, at the beginning of the exchange.

Why Do Puppies Like to Play Tug-of-War?

While only dogs really know why they love to tug, a human theory is that it is a part of the prey-killing sequence and as such is hardwired in and deeply satisfying to dog-kind. Dog trainers used to recommend against tug-of-war because it was thought to encourage dominance. Most modern trainers now think that this behavior has little to do with dominance,

and while it does need to be controlled, it need not be suppressed. Indeed, we are not very successful when we ask a predator such as the dog to give up predatory behavior, so suppression may not be possible. It is kinder and more successful to channel this kind of behavior. So play tug-of-war with your dog, but play it with these rules:

- The human starts the game, not the dog.

- The game ends when the human says it ends.
  (Teach the give command before starting tug games.)

- The game is suspended temporarily if the dog bites the

human, and it ends for the day if he bites the human a second time.

- Tug may be performed with only one designated toy.
  Note: small children cannot follow these rules reliably, so puppies who live with little kids should not be allowed to play tug-of-war.

Why Do Puppies Cry All Night Long?

Puppies don't cry all night long! Or, at least, they shouldn't. If your puppy is "distress vocalizing" to the extent that she cries all night long, it is probably because she is an infant from a very social species who is supposed to be sleeping in a warm pile of fat puppies and instead is alone in a kitchen or garage. Puppies generally do not do well if they are isolated during the night. It is unnatural for them.

Encourage your puppy to sleep through the night by having her sleep in the bedroom with her human pack members. She needs to be crated or otherwise confined at first to prevent housebreaking errors, destructive chewing, and engaging in other *Midnight Games*.

Why Do Puppies Nip?

Puppies play puppy games, not human games, with humans. Makes sense, right? Where would a Chesapeake Bay retriever even get a Scrabble set? Of course a puppy is limited to playing dog games, such as wrestling, biting, chasing, tug-of-war, and keep away, until we teach him some others.

Also, dogs and humans, despite our closeness and mutual affection, often miscommunicate. Children particularly routinely mishandle puppies, increasing their risk of being nipped or even bitten.

For example, small children who reach over Puppy's head to pat him, then quickly pull their hand away, worried that they might get bitten, make their worry come true. The puppy cannot help but respond by biting at the moving fingers. If the child then squeals and runs, the puppy is triggered to chase and bite at clothing. So, what are parents to do?

The child and parents should participate in a gentle puppy kindergarten class with their puppy to get general help with their relationship with, and control of, the puppy. Parents should always supervise interactions between a child and a puppy. If an adult cannot supervise, the puppy should be crated or confined in a puppy-proofed area, but in any case, separated from the child. Allowing a puppy (or worse, an adult dog) to play unsupervised with a group of children is a recipe for disaster.

Puppies who are stressed by isolation, boredom, and lack of exercise are even more likely to be mouthy, so do ensure that you are meeting your puppy's basic needs. Then, if it is still necessary, try these suggestions when the puppy gets nippy:

- This is definitely a case where less is more, as far as punishment goes. If you grab the puppy's muzzle or shake your finger in his face as you say "No, no!" most puppies will be delighted at your attempt to wrestle back and will bite more and harder.
- Instead, when your puppy bites, say, "OW!" loudly, then immediately turn away from the puppy. Tuck your hands under

your arms, look at the sky and ignore the puppy for thirty seconds or so until the puppy is not making any bite attempts. (We call this the "be a tree" position, to help kids remember it.) Then turn to the puppy and have him run through two or three of the obedience commands you are working on in puppy school (come, sit, down, stay) then reward him. After many repetitions, your puppy will get the picture: if he bites, he loses his playmate.

Teach your puppy alternate games in which he can exercise and earn attention without being touched and tempted. Retrieving and hide-and-seek are good choices.

Why Do Puppies Guard Their Toys and Food?

Object guarding is a normal dog behavior. Dogs are predators who historically have had to work hard for their meals. Yeah, I know it is hard to look at a fluffy Lhasa Apso puppy, who seems more like a sock puppet than a wolf, and think *predator,* but predatory behavior is hardwired in dogs. It makes sense, then, that a dog's attitude is *It's good, it's mine—Keep Away!*

In fact, it is only surprising that more dogs don't guard more stuff more vigorously.

Dogs can be surprisingly gentle, but you cannot rely on that. If you want to be able to handle your dog's food and toys and remove items from her mouth if necessary, start working with her as a puppy. Prevention with puppies is relatively simple and fun compared to attempting to treat object guarding in a big, hostile dog (which is no fun at all).

Follow these steps to teach a puppy to give you her objects on command: Use a consistent cue, such as saying "give," then give the puppy a high value treat in trade for a boring toy. Make the toy nicer (by smearing it with peanut butter, for example) and give it back to the puppy. Repeat the exercise by trading treats for the toy many times. Then choose a slightly more interesting toy and do the exercise again. Gradually, with many repetitions, work through the puppy's toys, trading for increasingly more loved toys until she cheerfully gives you even the best stuff.

Practice the following exercise around your puppy's food bowl. Sit down with her when she eats, and hand-feed her kibble with your hand in her bowl. You can also start her off with only about one-quarter of her meal in her bowl, then while she is eating, approach her with another quarter of her ration, and tip it into her bowl. While she is munching that, you, the ever-helpful human, appear with a third quarter ration of the food and then the final quarter ration. The puppy learns to welcome your approaching her food bowl.

Note: Always be aware of the potential for aggression in a dog who is competing (as she sees it) for food or other valuable resources. Seek professional help if your puppy is tense or growly in any of these exercises, or if you have an adult dog who object guards.

Why Do Some Puppies Avoid Looking at People?

Puppies communicate with their fellow dogs—and attempt to communicate with us humans—largely with body language. For dogs, direct eye contact, or staring straight at another, is often a threat. If you have a retiring sort of puppy, he may not be able to handle you looking directly in his eyes, even if you mean it lovingly. He may need to defer to you by averting his gaze, glancing away, or even, if he is particularly meek, turning his body away from you a little.

A meek puppy may require a little special nurturing—not babying—

because he needs to be brought out with a bit of extra work and insight on the owner's part. A good puppy kindergarten instructor can help you understand your gentle puppy's special needs.

Why Do Puppies Stick Their Rear-Ends Up in the Air?

The play bow is often accompanied by a play face in which the dog seems to be smiling. Her eyes shine, her mouth is open in a cheerful pant, and she looks as inviting as she feels!

In general, dogs lower themselves and attempt to look smaller when they want to encourage—or allow—another to come close. They may do this in submission with ears back, gaze averted, and an attitude of *come on over if you want because I am powerless to stop you, pose you no threat, and am so humble that I definitely don't need to be bitten.* Or they may do this more happily as with the play bow.

Dogs read human body language as if it were dog body language. This can lead to miscommunication, but with a little study of dog speak on the human's part, it can also lead to increased communication and increased fun! Try play bowing back to your puppy—most puppies find this hilarious!

Why Do Puppies Paw at Us?

Puppies paw to get attention. Some puppies do it in a pushy way, others gently, but the reward the puppy seeks is generally the same— to get the puppy's person to look at, touch, and talk to him. It usually works, too! Even being told to stop or being pushed away by a human who feels pestered usually entertains the puppy and keeps bringing him back to paw again. If you prefer that your puppy not do this, ignore the pawing completely. As soon as your puppy picks another activity, praise him quietly but sincerely.

Why Do Puppies Go on Frenzies?

This is one of the areas in which *dogs knowses and humans supposes*. Most people find their puppy's running "racetracks" around the house at absolute top speed, ears streaming, tail flattened, bumping into things as she races, very funny indeed. This particular aspect of puppy behavior, while mysterious, seems to be self-limiting and entirely benign. The appropriate response usually is to stand back and laugh. Soon, your exhausted puppy, tongue hanging, will finish the "race" and flop at your feet. Other aspects of dealing with the active dog are less amusing.

Expect your speed racer to be at her worst—most mouthy and most demanding—at dawn and at dusk. These are natural activity peak times for dogs. Plan exercise and training sessions for these times. Also plan to have puppy pacifier toys such as a Kong or sterilized bone stuffed with peanut butter available.

Why Do Puppies Learn So Quickly?

Youngsters of any "advanced" species are designed to be learning machines. A puppy investigates, explores, experiments, memorizes, and makes decisions about how to manipulate his humans at an impressive, even alarming, rate. It is not necessary or desirable to wait until he grows up before taking a puppy to training. A puppy is mostly a blank slate (there is some "genetic scribbling" there—he comes hardwired to chase stuff, wag his tail, and so on), but soon your training goals will be competing with his. Take your puppy to puppy kindergarten now!

If your puppy seems to be a little slow, well, you probably can't blame the puppy for this one. When puppies learn slowly it's usually because their humans are not being good teachers.

Some tips for being a good puppy professor:

- Break each learning task down into little bits.

- Reward every success.

- Reward with something the puppy wants (such as food, food, food, toys, play, etc...).

- Practice, practice, practice!

PENELOPE MILNE is a member of the Association of Pet Dog Trainers and the owner and principal of *DubDubDog* in Laguna Beach, California, where she has spent the last twenty years specializing in kind ways to train animals and their humans. Penny also acts as consultant to veterinary practices and animal welfare groups and leads presentations to kennel clubs, community associations, and other organizations. Born in Scotland, Penny now lives in Laguna Beach with her standard poodle, Colin; two cats, Rupert and Nassau; an elderly bunny, named Beth; and a mixed-breed human, Carroll-Oliver.